Minnesota Fish Species

Game Fish & Panfish

Billy Grinslott & Kinsey Marie Books

ISBN -9781965098783

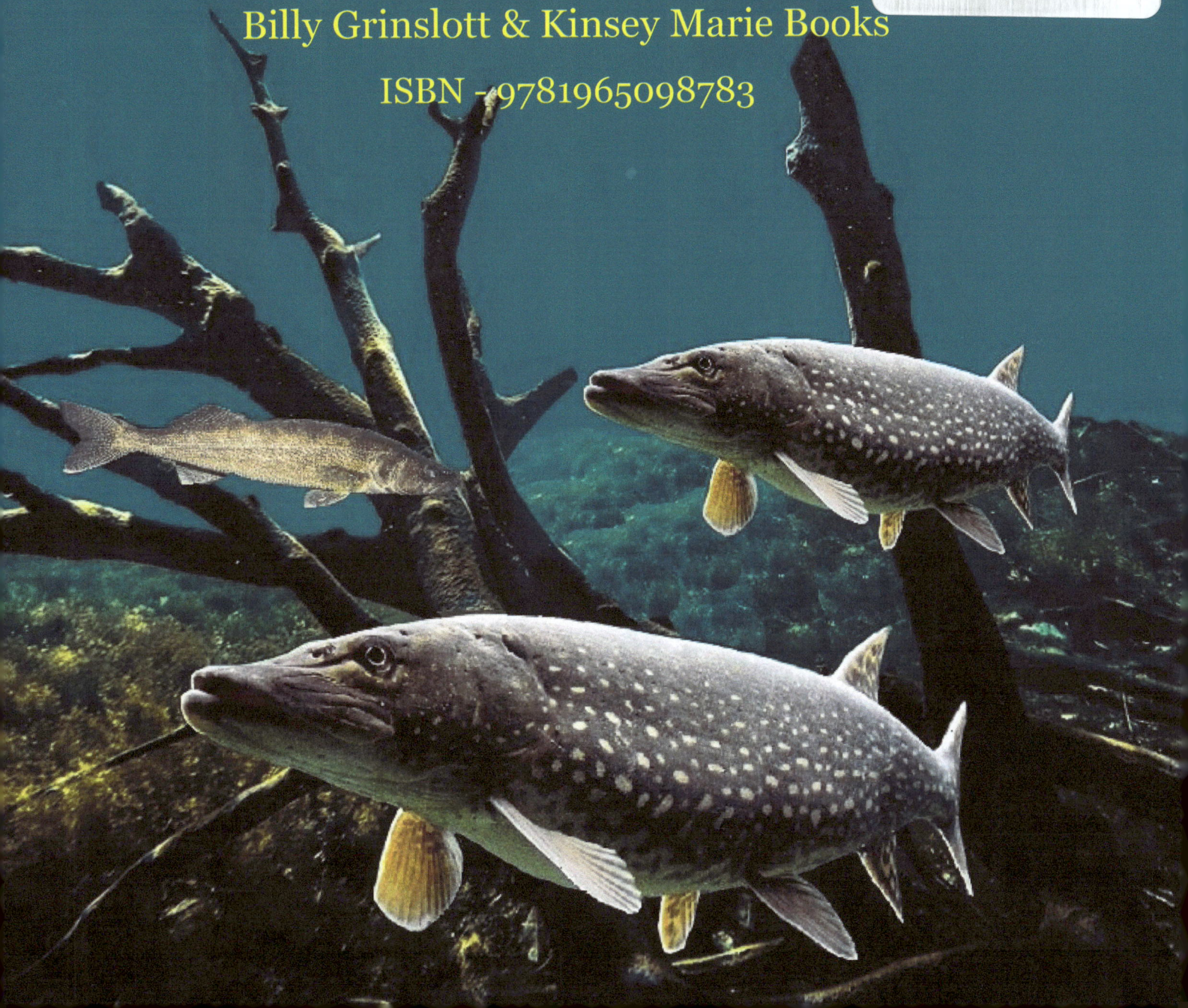

Creek Chubs and Golden Shiners are two types of minnows that are considered panfish. There are several types of shiners. Many people will use them as bate to catch larger fish. Creek chubs are silver in color and golden shiner have a gold color. There are also many types of silver shiners.

Ruffe fish have a perch-shaped body with walleye-like markings. They can survive in a variety of conditions, including fresh and brackish waters, and varying temperatures and depths. Ruffe fish are primarily bottom feeders, consuming aquatic insects, insect larvae, and small invertebrates. They are a small fish. Adult ruffe are typically 3 to 5 inches long but can grow up to 9 inches.

Longear sunfish are small, thin-bodied fish with a unique long ear flap on their gill cover, that how they got their name long ear. They are often mistaken for a pumpkinseed. They have an olive to rusty-brown back, a bright orange belly. They typically reach a length of 4.5 inches. They are mostly active during the day and inactive at night.

The Green Sunfish is blue green in color. It has yellow flecks on both its scales and some parts of its sides. The Green Sunfish also has broken blue stripes which is why some people confuse it with the Bluegill. Green Sunfish are very adaptable, they can live in any body of water that has vegetation or weeds. Green sunfish are opportunistic feeders, consuming insects, small fish, and other invertebrates.

Orange spotted sunfish are mostly found in floodplains of the United States of the Great Lakes. Its beautiful shiny silvery-blue body has reddish-orange spots, which give it its name, orange spotted sunfish. They are usually found in southern Muunesota but are too small to be popular with anglers. Their average length is 3 inches. They are a small fish.

The Warmouth is a member of the Rock Bass, Green Sunfish and Bluegill family. They can survive in low oxygen environments while other fish cannot. Warmouth can thrive in muddy water, when other fish can't. Warmouth are often confused with rock bass. The difference between the two is in the anal fin: warmouth have three spines on the anal fin ray and rock bass have six spines.

The bluegill also considered a sunfish is the most popular fish to fish for. They are called pan fish because they are about the size of a frying pan. Bluegills love to eat insects and bugs. They have good vision and rely on their keen eyesight to feed. Three types in this group are the Bluegill, Sunfish, and Pumpkinseed.

The Pumpkinseed is also known as pond perch, sun perch, and punky's sunfish. It can be found in numerous lakes, ponds, and rivers. It is their body shape resembling the seed of a pumpkin, that inspired their name. Pumpkinseed sunfish have speckles on their orangish colored sides and back, with a yellow to orange belly and chest. They are active during the day and rest at night near the bottom or in shelter areas.

The two most famous perches are the common perch and the yellow perch. The yellow perch has a brilliant greenish yellow color with orange fins. The yellow perch is the biggest one and can grow to a size of 18 inches. It's also known as the jumbo perch. The other type of perch is the white perch. The largest yellow perch recorded in Minnesota weighed 3 pounds, 4 ounces.

The Rock Bass is not actually a bass but a member of the sunfish family. The biggest Rock Bass ever caught on record weighs about three pounds and was a little over one foot long. Rock bass like waters with rocky vegetated areas, that's how they got their name.

There are two main types of crappies. The white crappie and the black crappie. They are also members of the sunfish family. The difference between the white and black crappie is one has dark spots and the other has dark lines and is lighter in color. The white crappie has six dorsal fin spines, whereas the black crappie has eight dorsal fin spines. The white crappie can grow bigger and more of the bigger white crappie are caught in North America.

The White sucker fish has the same mouth as a carp. They got their name because their mouth is like a suction cup. They normally are bottom feeders and suck their food from the bottom of the lake. Many people use sucker fish to fish for northern pike and other big game fish. The largest sucker fish caught in Minnesota is the Blue Sucker, with a weight of 14 pounds and 2 ounces and a length of 30.4 inches.

Flathead Catfish, their body is wide but flattened and very low in height. Both eyes are on the top of the flattened head, giving excellent vision to see upward. Flathead catfish live mainly in large bodies of water like big rivers and reservoirs. They prefer deep pools. The largest flathead catfish caught in Minnesota was 52.5-inches long and weighed 80 pounds.

The black bullhead and yellow bullhead are part of the catfish family. They usually only grow to about 10 inches long. They use their whiskers to help find food. The bullhead is the most common member of the catfish family. Bullheads live in the water containing low oxygen levels. They can survive on low oxygen areas, where other fish can't.

There are several species of catfish. The Channel Catfish are the most fished catfish species with around 8 million anglers fishing for them per year. Channel Catfish have very few teeth and swallow their food whole. Channel catfish live in freshwater rivers, lakes, streams, and ponds. Catfish can live in low oxygen water, like bullheads. The largest channel catfish caught in Minnesota weighed 38 pounds and was 44 inches long.

Bowfins can breathe both air and water, putting them at an advantage in low-oxygen waters. Bowfins are often described as prehistoric relics. This is because species can be traced to fossils from the Cretaceous, Eocene and Jurassic period. The Minnesota state record for a bowfin, also known as a dogfish, is 11.25 pounds.

White Bass range in color from a silvery white to a pale green. Their backs are mostly black, while their sides and belly are pale with stripes running along them. White Bass are related to Striped Bass and called wipers. The largest certified white bass caught in Minnesota, by weight, weighed 4 pounds, 8 ounces.

Yellow bass, scientifically known as Morone mississippiensis, are a relatively small, schooling fish with a golden-yellow body and dark stripes, often found in rivers and lakes, particularly in areas with dense vegetation. The average size for this fish is 12 inches in length and one pound in weight. They are also known as rockfish, streaker, and yellow belly. The largest yellow bass caught in Minnesota weighed 1 pound, 3 ounces.

Lake whitefish are related to salmon and trout. They are known for their deep-bodied, silvery appearance and are a major part of the Great Lakes ecosystem. They typically grow to 17-22 inches and range from 1.5-4 pounds. Whitefish are a popular and valuable commercial fish, generating the greatest income for Great Lakes commercial fisheries. Lake whitefish are also known as Lake Superior whitefish, whiting, and shad. The largest lake whitefish caught in Minnesota, and the current state record, weighed 13 pounds, 9 ounces.

There are two different species of Gar, the Longnose gar, and Alligator gar. The Long Nose Gar got its name because of its long mouth that looks like an alligator's mouth. The alligator gar is one of the biggest freshwater fish growing up to 10 feet long. The world record for a catch was set at 327 pounds. The largest gar caught in Minnesota, and the state record, is a longnose gar weighing 16 pounds and 12 ounces.

Lake Sturgeons have sharp spines on their back, so be careful when handling them. Instead of scales, sturgeon skin is covered in bony plates called scutes, which can be very sharp on young sturgeon. Sturgeons have been around since the dinosaur days. Sturgeons mostly live in large, freshwater lakes and rivers. Their average lifespan is 50 to 60 years. The biggest sturgeon caught in Minnesota, and a state catch-and-release record, was a 78-inch, 120-pound lake sturgeon.

The burbot, also known as the eel pout. They get their name because they have a serpent-like or eel-like body. They can wrap their tail around things. There's nothing to worry about if you catch one, they may try to wrap their tail around your arm, but they are harmless. Burbots are adapted to cold water and are found in large, cold rivers, lakes, and reservoirs, primarily preferring freshwater habitats. Burbots are also known as eelpout, lingcod, and lawyer. The largest burbot, or eelpout, ever caught in Minnesota weighed in at 19 pounds, 11 ounces.

Male freshwater drum make a rumbling or grunting sound by contracting muscles along their air bladder walls. They have large, ivory-like ear bones that can be up to an inch in diameter, which Native Americans used as necklaces or bracelets and sometimes referred to as the lucky stones. Freshwater drum are primarily bottom feeders, spending much of their time near the bottom of lakes and rivers in search of food. The largest freshwater drum caught in Minnesota weighed 35 pounds and 3.2 ounces.

Buffalo Fish are sometimes confused with carp. Buffalo fish have a downward-facing mouth, capable of sucking bits of food out of the silt and sand on the bottom. They have broad bodies, blunt heads, and silvery gray or brown scales. Buffalo fish are members of the suckerfish family. The largest certified Bigmouth Buffalo fish caught in Minnesota weighed 41 pounds and 11 ounces.

Carp have long been an important food fish to humans. Carp are bottom feeders for the most part and their mouth is made like a suction cup, so they can suck food off the bottom. Carp are good for a lake because they help clean the bottom of the lake. The largest invasive carp ever recorded in Minnesota was a 61.7-pound, 47.5-inch bighead carp.

Brook trout are characterized by their olive-green bodies with pale, worm-like markings, red spots with bluish halos, and orange-red fins with white and black edges. They can grow up to 12 inches in length. Brook trout are cold-water fish that prefer clean, clear, and cold streams, lakes, and ponds. The largest brook trout caught in Minnesota weighed 6 pounds, 5 ounces.

The lake trout is one of the biggest of the trout family. The biggest lake trout caught was 72 pounds. Lake trout like to live in lakes that are deep. They like being in the cool water in the deep parts of a lake. They have been reported to live up to 70 years in some Canadian lakes. The largest lake trout caught in Minnesota weighed 43 pounds and 8 ounces.

Brown trout can live up to 20 years. Brown trout have higher tolerance for warmer waters than either brook or rainbow trout. Brown trout can be found on almost every continent except Antarctica, and many can be found living in the ocean. The current Minnesota state record for a brown trout is 16 pounds, 12 ounces, Length 31 3/8 inches.

The rainbow trout gets its name because of its brilliant colors. Rainbow trout populations are good indicators of water pollution because they can only survive in clean waters. They like to live in rivers and streams. Rainbow trout rank among the top five most sought game fish in North America. The largest rainbow trout caught in Minnesota weighed 16 pounds and 6 ounces.

Minnesota has salmon, specifically in Lake Superior, where Chinook, Coho, and pink salmon are found. They are popular for fishing, with some streams getting runs of these species, as well as steelhead, browns, and splake. Chinook also known as the king salmon are the most widespread Salmon in North America. The largest Chinook salmon caught in Minnesota, tied for the state record, weighed 33 pounds, 4 ounces.

The largemouth bass is the most sought-after bass in North America. Largemouth bass live in just about every lake in North America. They have great hearing and can hear a crayfish crawling on the bottom of the lake. The Minnesota state record for a largemouth bass is an 8-pounds, 15-ounces.

Smallmouth bass have a smaller mouth than the largemouth bass. They also have different markings and are lighter in color. They don't live in most lakes because they prefer living in colder water. They are typically found in the northern states in America because the water is cooler. The current world record smallmouth is an 11-pound, 15-ounce fish caught in Dale Hollow Lake. The largest smallmouth bass caught in Minnesota weighed 8 pounds and was 23.5-inches long.

The sauger is part of the walleye family. There are 2 different types of saugers. The normal sauger and the suageye. The saugeye is a mix of the sauger and walleye. The suageye have white eyes just like the walleye. The sauger and suageye are smaller than the walleye. Saugers are more likely to be found in large rivers with deep pools but are also found in lakes. The largest sauger caught in Minnesota weighed 6 pounds, 2 ounces.

Another breed of the Muskie is the tiger muskie. The tiger muskie is a cross between the northern pike and muskie. They grow larger and faster than normal muskies and northern pikes. The tiger muskie got its name because it has tiger like stripes. Tiger Muskies are very rare and hard to catch. The largest tiger muskie caught in Minnesota weighed 34 pounds, 12 ounces with a length of 51 inches.

The muskellunge called the Musky or Muskie for short is one of the biggest game fish in freshwater lakes. The largest on record was 69 pounds, 15 ounces. The Muskie likes to live in cooler water and can be found in most lakes in the upper part of north America. Anglers look at Muskellunges as trophy fish. They are hard to catch, there's a saying that it takes a thousand casts to catch one. The largest muskellunge caught in Minnesota, and the current state record for a catch-and-release muskie, is a 58.25-inch long.

The walleye got its name because of its white looking eyes. Their eyes collect light, even in low light conditions. This means they can see in the dark. Because they can see in the dark, they mostly feed at night. During the daytime their eyes are very sensitive, so they usually head for deeper water or shady places. Walleye like to live in cooler water and are normally found in the upper part of North America. The largest walleye ever caught in Minnesota weighed 17 pounds and 8 ounces and 35 ¾ inches long.

The Northern Pike is one of the most sought-after fish for anglers. It got its name because it likes to live in cooler water mainly in the northern states of North America. The northern pike is a very aggressive predator. They don't like to live in groups with other fish, they are very territorial and like to live alone. Their behavior is closely affected by weather conditions. The state record for a catch-and-release northern pike is 46.25 inches lomg.

Fun Facts About Minnesota Fish

1 - The walleye is Minnesota's official state fish, designated in 1965. The state record walleye is 17 pounds and 8 ounces.

2 - Minnesota is home to 162 species of fish, 141 are native.

3 - Lake sturgeon are the largest fish in Minnesota, with some weighing over 100 pounds and living over 150 years.

4 - Minnesota's muskies are bigger and more widespread due to stocking programs and catch-and-release efforts.

5 - Besides walleye, other popular game fish include bass, catfish, crappie, sunfish, and perch.

6 - Northern pike are exciting to catch, readily attacking lures, especially larger plugs and spoons.

7 - Minnesota has brook, brown, and rainbow trout.

8 - There are over 18,000 miles of fishable rivers and streams.

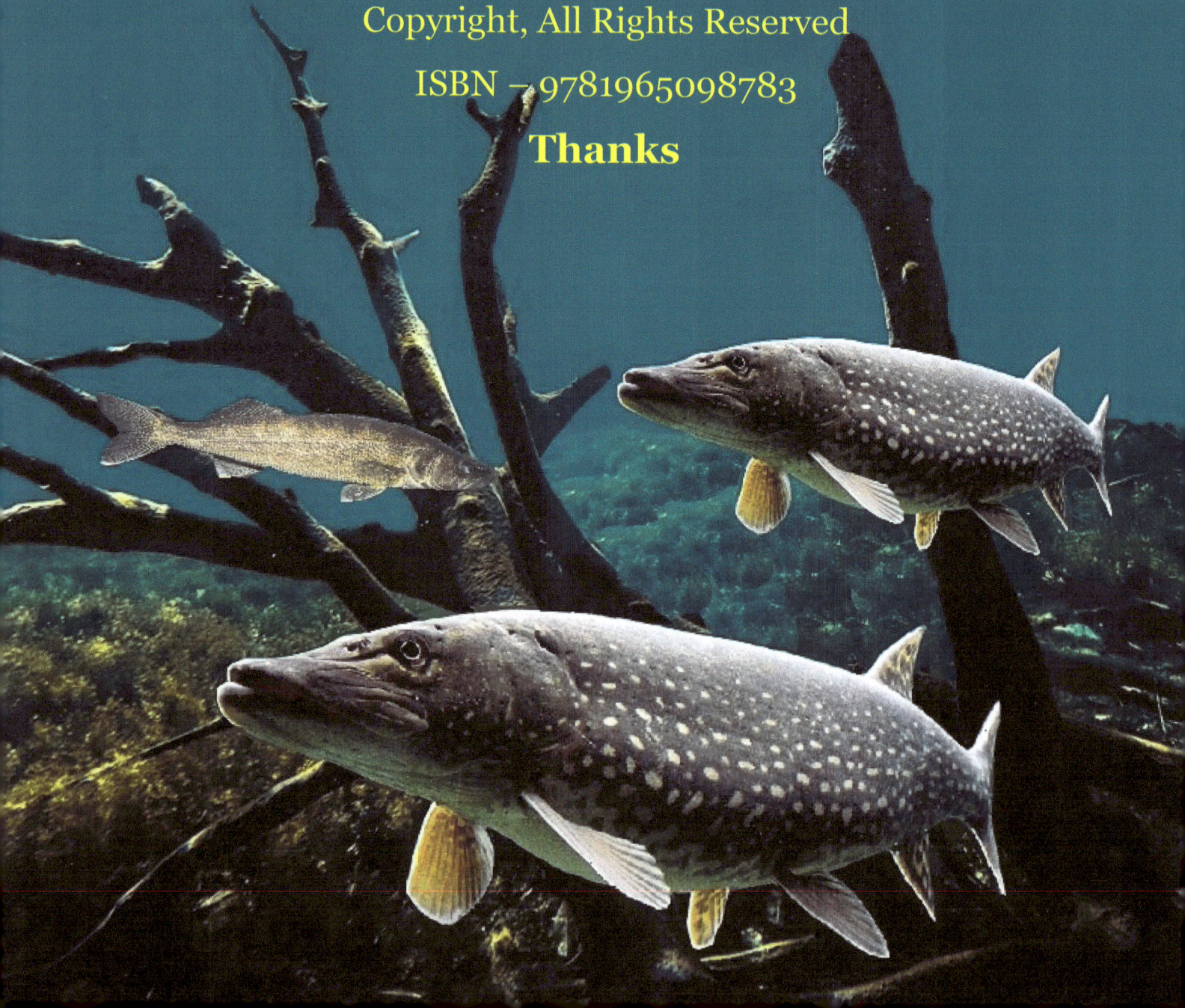

Author Page

Billy Grinslott & Kinsey Marie Books

Copyright, All Rights Reserved

ISBN – 9781965098783

Thanks

Author Page

Billy Grinslott & Kinsey Marie Books

Copyright, All Rights Reserved

ISBN – 9781965098998

Thanks

Fun Facts About Nebraska Fish

1 - Channel Catfish is the official state fish of Nebraska and is found in nearly many bodies of water in the state.

2 - The largest fish ever caught in Nebraska was a paddlefish weighing 113 pounds, 4 ounces.

3 - Nebraska is home to over 100 fish species, with 78 considered to be native.

4 - The state has records for various fish, like the blue cat 100 lbs. 8 oz. channel catfish 31 lbs. 13 oz. flathead catfish 89 lbs.

5 - The most frequently caught fish in Nebraska is arguably the sunfish, particularly the bluegill.

6 – A record goldfish was caught in Nebraska. It weighed 6 pounds and 12 ounces.

7 - Smelling and tasting. Fish use their nostrils to smell, and catfish use their barbels or whiskers to taste.

www.ingramcontent.com/pod-product-compliance
Lightning Source LLC
Chambersburg PA
CBHW060851270326
41934CB00002B/92